MULTIMEDIA ARTIST AND ANIMATOR

Published in the United States of America by Cherry Lake Publishing
Ann Arbor, Michigan
www.cherrylakepublishing.com

Content Adviser: Stephanie Boxold, Motion Graphic Artist at MLB Advanced Media
Reading Adviser: Marla Conn MS, Ed., Literacy specialist, Read-Ability, Inc.

Photo Credits: © wavebreakmedia/Shutterstock, cover, 1, 24; © Sean Pavone/Shutterstock, 5; © Atelier Sommerland/
Shutterstock, 6; © Rawpixel.com/Shutterstock, 7; ©Daniel SIMON / Contributor/Getty, 8; © George Dolgikh/Shutterstock,
11; © Kzenon/Shutterstock, 12; © Photos 12 / Alamy Stock Photo, 14; © Dikiiy/Shutterstock, 16; © Moviestore collection Ltd /
Alamy Stock Photo, 18, ©Mushakesa/Shutterstock, 21; © Zoran Karapancev/Shutterstock, 22; © Geber86/istock, 27;
©StockLite/Shutterstock, 28

Library of Congress Cataloging-in-Publication Data
Names: Labrecque, Ellen, author.
Title: Multimedia artist and animator / Ellen Labrecque.
Description: Ann Arbor : Cherry Lake Publishing, [2016] |
Series: Cool vocational careers | Audience: Grades 4 to 6. |
   Includes bibliographical references and index.
Identifiers: LCCN 2015046659| ISBN 9781634710640 (hardcover) | ISBN 9781634712620 (pbk.) |
   ISBN 9781634711630 (pdf) | ISBN 9781634713610 (ebook)
Subjects: LCSH: Animation (Cinematography)—Vocational guidance—Juvenile literature. |
   Computer animation—Vocational guidance—Juvenile literature. |
   Multimedia (Art)—Vocational guidance--Juvenile literature.
Classification: LCC TR897.5 .L33 2016 | DDC 741.5/8023—dc23
LC record available at http://lccn.loc.gov/2015046659

Cherry Lake Publishing would like to acknowledge the work of the Partnership for 21st Century Learning.
Please visit *www.p21.org* for more information.

Printed in the United States of America
Corporate Graphics

ABOUT THE AUTHOR

Ellen Labrecque is a freelance writer living in Yardley, Pennsylvania. Previously, she was a senior editor at *Sports Illustrated Kids*. Ellen loves to travel and then learn about new places and people she can write about in her books.

TABLE OF CONTENTS

CHAPTER 1

Life Is Art 4

CHAPTER 2

Creative Central 10

CHAPTER 3

Becoming a Multimedia Artist and Animator 20

CHAPTER 4

Creating the Future 26

THINK ABOUT IT... 30
FOR MORE INFORMATION...31
GLOSSARY 32
INDEX... 32

Life Is Art

Have you ever walked around a big city? Everywhere you look, you probably see giant billboards and giant television screens. You see store signs, and logos on buildings and in windows.

Think about being at school. What art do you see in the hallways, in your classroom, or in the offices? Did you make some of this art yourself?

Art is all around us. Some of it is for entertainment. Some of it is on advertisements, trying to convince you to buy things. Art comes in many **media**, including paintings, sculptures, **animations**, and **art installations**. When you see a poster in your classroom, you're seeing something made by an artist.

Advertising is just one of many types of art.

Many computer programs let you work on illustrations.

Designers use programs to change colors and shapes of images.

Art is on your computer. When you start up the computer, you often see a logo. An artist created that logo. At a Web site, you see art and designs. Some are animated, like moving cartoons. Others remain still, like a photograph. Even the Web site itself has been designed. Designers arrange words, pictures, and drawings in ways that make the site fun and interesting to look at.

There are many **multimedia** artists and animators who create the **images** and designs you see every day. Many opportunities exist in this field. You can work in advertising. You

Computers have come a long way since the 1990s.

can work as a multimedia artist in film or television. You can work on video games. The multimedia artists and animators who do this work have interesting, exciting jobs.

21st Century Content

The search engine Google runs a contest every year. It asks students in kindergarten through grade 12 to create a Google doodle. The winning doodle is featured on Google's home page. These doodles are "meant to surprise and delight people" when they visit the home page. That's what the inventors of the contest wrote at the Web site. Do you want to enter this contest? Go to www.google.com/doodle4google to find out how!

CHAPTER 2

Creative Central

Marie Dumlao is a multimedia artist and a photographer in Philadelphia, Pennsylvania. Marie works on many kinds of projects. She works with films, videos, texts, and other media, including photography and video. On her Web site, Marie says her art involves drawing "what-if" scenarios. This means she puts many different media together, to see what she can create in the end.

Marie has **exhibited** her work all over the world, from Philadelphia and New York to Tokyo, Japan, and Berlin, Germany. Her exhibits are a combination of still photographs, video, and even sound pieces.

"I don't really stick with one medium," Marie says. "Sometimes I even do sculptures along with other media— even sound pieces."

Painting is just one medium available to artists.

Some multimedia artists focus on mixing music and video soundtracks.

Marie works in a studio that's inside her home. She has a corner set up for her young son, so he can create alongside her. She also teaches studio art at a community college. The classes she has taught include Video Study Production, Art History, and Sound Design for Film and Video. When Marie isn't teaching, her schedule varies. If she has an upcoming exhibit, she will sometimes work throughout the entire night. If she doesn't have a show, she teaches herself new skills. Or she looks for new ideas by watching a film or reading a book.

Marie has also done some work for other people. She has edited **trailers** for films. She has created **sound design** for videos. She says she is always teaching herself new skills as a multimedia artist, whether taking a class or following a **tutorial** on her computer.

The animator and story artist Scott Clark has worked for almost 20 years for Pixar, a computer animation film studio. *Animate* means "bring life to." Using **3D** computer programs, studios such as Pixar are able to make characters come to life by moving shapes and models in a 3D environment. Scott helps create these movies by drawing the characters and their environment, which are then animated in 3D software. Scott has

Monsters University is a popular movie from Pixar.

helped animate movies such as *Toy Story II, Cars, Finding Nemo,* and *Monsters University.* These movies are made using 3D computer programs. They can take as long as four to five years to complete—it's a complicated process!

The team at Pixar starts by sketching **scenes** on a storyboard. "Storyboards are drawn by story artists for the purpose of pre-visualizing the film," says one animator from Pixar. That means forming a picture of it in your mind. "They are placed side by side in sequence, so that they convey scenes and deliver a rough sense of how the story unfolds." Each storyboard image has a piece of the script alongside it, visually representing that specific part of the movie. During the rest of the making of the movie, the animators will constantly refer to the storyboards for every camera move and scene.

Thousands and thousands of storyboards are created for movies. The movie *Monsters University* had 227,246 storyboards! After storyboards are created, the next step is making an animatic, which is a moving storyboard. It is very rough animation that determines the timing and how the characters and environment move. It's usually done in **2D**, before getting fully developed in 3D.

Sometimes multimedia artists need to discuss their plans with the rest of the team.

Next, the art department takes the sketches and creates more detailed art illustrating the fictional world and its characters. This is called **concept art**, and sometimes it might be created before or during the making of the storyboards. The artists brainstorm several versions of each character, object, and building, and then the team picks the strongest ones. The art department also designs **sets** and adds color and lighting.

Then, while looking at the concept art, Pixar's animators use software to create 3D computer models of characters and sets. This is a little like molding things out of clay, but digitally. They also add **texture** to these models. This makes each image look like it would feel a certain way if you touched it. Texture also includes the colors of the objects in the scene, and how these colors reflect the light.

Life and Career Skills

Here are some of the jobs you can do as a multimedia artist or animator.

- *Help create an animated film like* Inside Out *or* Toy Story *(3D animation)*
- *Create a cartoon like* Phineas and Ferb *(2D animation)*
- *Design new video game graphics (3D animation)*
- *Work in advertising and help create commercials, billboards, and online content (2D and 3D animation)*
- *Animate graphics of team logos and matchups during sports games (2D and 3D animation)*
- *Work as a visual effects artist, adding special effects to live-action film to be used in movies and commercials*
- *Work on your own personal art and exhibit it all over the world*

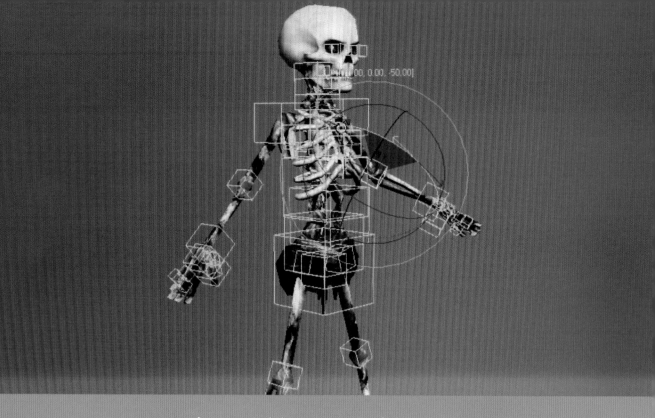

Avars control the movements of characters.

The team also has to decide how to light the scene's environment. Is this part of the story taking place indoors or outdoors? Is it day or night? Where do the shadows fall? These things make a difference.

Using these 3D models, the animators also create movement and expressions. This process is called rigging. Each character is given a basic skeleton. Then the designers add controls, sometimes called "avars." Avars are used to make the characters move their bodies and faces in small ways. Woody, from the *Toy Story* movies, has 100 avars in his face alone!

[21ST CENTURY SKILLS LIBRARY]

Now that the avars have been assigned, the animators get to use them. They use thousands of keyframes, or set positions that begin and end, to make a character walk and talk. An animator may spend months perfecting the way a character speaks his or her **dialogue**. By using this computer program, the Pixar team brings the entire movie to life!

Lastly, the pieces of animation become the final movie in a process called rendering. Depending on the amount of data, this may take days, weeks, or even months. Finally, all that hard work pays off! The movie is done.

CHAPTER 3

Becoming a Multimedia Artist and Animator

There are many ways to become a multimedia artist or animator. Multimedia artists may have had graphic design training at a 2-year or 4-year college. Marie received a Bachelor of Fine Arts degree in studio art and art history. After earning her degree, she worked as a photo researcher at a magazine in New York City. She was also shooting her own photos and getting them published in books and magazines. She then went back to school and earned a Master of Fine Arts degree in studio art.

Marie says drawing is very important. If you love to draw, keep at it. Whatever schooling you decide on, drawing will always be the best way to prepare for a career as a multimedia artist or animator. She also says it is important to be a part of a bigger art

An artist who draws characters needs a good understanding
of the human body.

community. And, she adds, always be curious about the world around you! "Creative people can inspire one another," she says.

Scott grew up drawing cartoons and watching Bugs Bunny on television. He went to the Rhode Island School of Design for college and studied illustration and design. When he graduated, he was hired as an **intern** at Pixar. He has worked there ever since.

"I tell students to take life-drawing classes, animation classes," says Scott about becoming an animator. "It also helps to have a good sense of humor, a good sense of story."

Not all art is a flat picture. This art project is many chairs hung from the ceiling.

There are many ways to prepare to become a multimedia artist or animator. The key is to keep at it. Sketch, watch things, and think about what you see. Think about what looks cool. Think about why it looks cool to you. Ask yourself what about it holds your attention. Think about how you might change it. Study different kinds of art. Museums can be great places to see modern art as well as art that was created hundreds or even thousands of years ago. Art is about seeing things and creating things. Look at things and make things. That is how you become an artist.

Life and Career Skills

Different colleges are better than others depending on what you want to study. If you want to study multimedia art or animation, you can't beat these five schools:

1. *California Institute of the Arts in Valencia, California*
2. *University of Southern California in Los Angeles, California*
3. *Savannah College of Art and Design in Savannah, Georgia*
4. *Rhode Island School of Design in Providence, Rhode Island*
5. *University of California, Los Angeles in Los Angeles, California*

Animators are always practicing with new computer programs.

Being an animator requires a lot of technical skills, too. People who work in 2D animation often use the Adobe programs After Effects, Flash, Photoshop, and Illustrator. For 3D animators, some important programs are Cinema 4D, Autodesk Maya, 3ds Max, and ZBrush. Animators often start learning these in high school and college, but they keep practicing all through their careers. A strong knowledge of these complex programs may help someone get a job, but there are also new techniques to learn, too.

Creating the Future

There's so much multimedia art and animation around us. They are constantly being created, and people will be needed to create more. Employment in multimedia art and animation will continue to grow, according to the U.S. government. There were about 68,900 multimedia artists and animators in the United States in 2012. By 2022, the government believes there will be more than 73,000. There are many talented, creative people in the world. This will always be a field with a lot of competition. It will take both talent and determination to find work.

The work will change as new technologies develop. Computer software will make some things easier. It will add new kinds of things to do. But for the most part, the role of artists and animators will stay the same. They will continue to carefully

Many companies have at least one multimedia artist working for them.

Tablets are a useful tool for multimedia artists.

observe the world. They will probably always have a pencil and paper close by. They will continue to practice different ways to present images.

They will also continue to create new ways to show objects and ideas. No matter the technology, multimedia artists and animators will keep doing what they've done for many years. They will communicate through images.

21st Century Content

According to the U.S. government, multimedia artists and animators earn between $34,860 and $113,470 a year. The industries that offer the highest salaries for these jobs are:

1. Motion picture and video: $72,690
2. Software publishers: $62,310
3. Advertising, public relations, and related services: $60,220
4. Computer systems design and related services: $58,950
Why do you think animators in the film industry earn the most?

Think About It

Visit www.pixar.com and click on the Behind the Scenes tab. What can you learn about how some of the big Pixar movies are made? Click on the Careers tab, too. Do any of the jobs listed sound like something you'd like to do someday?

Taking acting classes can be an important step on the journey to becoming an animator. Why do you think this is the case? How would knowing how to act help you as an animator?

Watch your favorite sports team play a live game on TV, or find a video of them playing online. Do they have a logo or mascot? An artist designed that. What about when players' statistics are shown? Or what about when a moment is replayed in slow motion? Watch it for a few minutes and make a list of every time you see an example of animation.

For More Information

BOOKS

Katz, Jason. *Funny! Twenty-Five Years of Laughter from the Pixar Story Room*. San Francisco: Chronicle Books, 2014.

Schwake, Susan. *Art Lab for Kids: 52 Creative Adventures in Drawing, Painting, Printmaking, Paper, and Mixed Media for Budding Artists of All Ages*. Beverly, MA: Quarry Books, 2012.

Temple, Kathryn. *Art for Kids: Drawing*. New York: Sterling Children's Books, 2014.

WEB SITES

Artyfactory
www.artyfactory.com
This site offers free art and design lessons.

Pixar
www.pixar.com
Learn all about how Pixar makes its magic films.

GLOSSARY

animations (an-ih-MAY-shuhnz) pieces of art that make something look alive, such as a cartoon character

art installations (AHRT in-stuh-LAY-shuhnz) performances, sculptures, or other art created and shown in the same place

concept art (KAHN-sept AHRT) different versions of characters, objects, or buildings that animators choose the final designs from

dialogue (DYE-uh-lawg) conversation, especially in a play, movie, TV show, or book

exhibited (ig-ZIB-it-id) presented an art show to the public

images (IM-ih-jiz) forms, appearances, or pictures of things

intern (IN-turn) someone who is learning a skill or job by working with an expert in that field

media (MEE-dee-uh) materials or techniques an artist uses

multimedia (muhl-ti-MEE-dee-uh) using several different media at the same time, such as text, sound, and video

observe (uhb-ZURV) to see or watch

scenes (SEENZ) parts of a film or show that take place at a particular time and location

sets (SEHTS) the places or areas in which the action of a film or show is recorded

sound design (SOUND dih-ZINE) the process of producing and controlling elements of sound

texture (TEKS-chur) the way something feels, or the look of the way it would feel

3D (THREE-dee) having or seeming to have the three dimensions of length, width, and height

trailers (TRAY-lurs) groups of scenes that are used to advertise movies

tutorial (too-TOR-ee-uhl) a short course in which you learn to do a particular thing

2D (TOO-dee) having or seeming to have the two dimensions of length and width

INDEX

animatics, 15
animators
    future of, 26–29
    how to become one, 20–25
    real-life, 13–19
    what they do, 4–9
    what they earn, 29
avars, 18–19

concept art, 16

education, 20–21, 23

models, 3D, 16–17, 18
movies, 13–19
multimedia artists
    how to become one, 20–25
    real-life, 10–13
    what they do, 4–9, 17
    what they earn, 29

Pixar, 13–19, 21

rendering, 19
rigging, 18

software, 13, 15, 24, 25, 26
story artists, 13–19
storyboards, 15, 16

technology, 26, 28
texture, 17

video, 9, 12, 13